HOW TO COACH
DIFFICULT
PEOPLE
in six steps

Kris Plachy, MA, Master Coach

Illustrated by Steven Hall | stevenhalldesign.com

LEADERSHIP COACH
— INC —

How to Coach the Difficult Person

The truth is, we all encounter people in our lives and in our work we consider to be difficult. It is as they are; unavoidable. In fact, it's so common it really is quite astonishing how challenging it is for people to deal with difficult people. It's almost as if we expect there not to be difficult people and then when we interact with one, we are shocked they exist. It's really quite the contrary. Difficult people are everywhere.

This guide is for people who manage or coach people who are considered 'difficult.' There is a high probability that all managers have to coach someone on their team that may create challenges for other team members. The goal of this guide is to give managers and coaches some clear, step-by-step guidance on how to unravel the difficult person from their difficult behavior and create self-awareness and (ultimately) change.

Who are the Difficult People?

For purposes of this guide, we will define difficult people as follows: Anyone who demonstrates behaviors that are considered to be challenging, insensitive, self-serving, rude, obnoxious, hurtful, overly-aggressive, overly-direct, unaccommodating, unsupportive, or any version of these.

In the workplace (just as it is in life), 'difficult' is a pretty subjective experience. What one person may experience as challenging, someone else may experience as spirited. What one person may experience as obnoxious, another may experience as passionate.

For managers and coaches, where we need to direct our attention is towards those people on our teams or in our organizations that are receiving multiple complaints and resistance from other employees. When the behavior of an employee perpetually impacts the ability of other employees to constructively complete their work, we (as leaders) must step in.

This guide is dedicated to coaching THAT difficult person. We created another guide called "5 Truths for Thinking About Difficult People," which is perfectly suited for employees to help themselves through the challenges of a difficult relationship.

Where Difficult Behavior Comes From

As a coach, it's imperative you understand where behavior comes from and how to help others change their own actions and outcomes.

The model outlined below demonstrates the root of all behavior:

CIRCUMSTANCE: Something happens in our world that we can prove (a conversation, an email, an experience, or an unexpected event) and cannot control.

THOUGHT: We define the circumstance in our mind. Whatever it is that happened (provable) we make it mean something with our thinking.

FEELING: How we think, drives how we feel. If we think something good, we feel positive emotion. If we think something negative, we experience uncomfortable or painful emotion.

ACTION / BEHAVIOR: How we feel drives the actions we take. If we feel negative emotions, we take negative action. If we feel positive feelings we take positive action.

RESULTS: What we do leads to the results we get. If we act engaged, excited and happy with others, we get one result. If we yell, dismiss, or are arrogant with others, we get another kind of result. The results we achieve are always in support of our originating thoughts.

When it comes to everyone (not just difficult people), how we experience one another is through behavior. So, difficult people demonstrate behaviors other people don't like. They may be negative or contrarian. They may be dismissive or rude. They may talk over people and not listen. They may be

CTFAR Model

CIRCUMSTANCES
can trigger

THOUGHTS
cause

FEELINGS
cause

ACTIONS
cause

RESULTS

Evidence

directive and non-collaborative. Essentially, as the coach you have to notice what their behavior is and then realize that behavior is caused by their feelings, which is caused by their thinking.

For example, a manager may be working with multiple deadlines.

This is provable or a **CIRCUMSTANCE**.

The manager's thought about these multiple deadlines may be, "I'm going to look bad if I don't get it all done."

This is their **THOUGHT**.

Because they think this thought, they feel helpless.

FEELING is an emotion or vibration in the body.

When they feel helpless, they lash out at the team for not doing enough work.

Lashing out is the **ACTION** or behavior that everyone else experiences.

When the manager lashes out at the team, this creates conflict amongst the team members and frankly, makes the manager look bad.

The **RESULT** is the manager gets support for the original thought, which is the manager actually ends up looking bad.

All thoughts we have will drive feelings and actions that create results, which support the originating thought.

If we want to change behavior and results, we must notice the thoughts we have that are driving our feelings, actions, and results.

As the coach, your best insight comes first from understanding and observing behavior. You can watch it and observe it. Once you've done so, you have to get to the CAUSE of the behavior. You have to understand (and help them to understand) what the thoughts are that are driving the outcomes they are getting.

Behavior is simply a window into the mind of your employee or client. We cannot tell or talk someone into new behavior. We have to help them understand why they act the way they do, when they act the way they do, in order for them to create sustainable, lasting behavior change.

6 Steps for Coaching The Difficult Person

Outlined in this guide is the recommended step-by-step process to follow when coaching a person who has been labeled as difficult. The practices included have been tested and proved out time and time again. When you decide to coach a difficult person, it is imperative you, as the coach, do your own due diligence to ensure your effectiveness as a coach. In most cases, people who have been labeled as difficult:

- **Have no idea they are acting in a way that is perceived as difficult.**

- **Do not intend to be difficult or hurtful or disruptive.**

- **Even if they do know they are thought of as difficult, they have not been given clear enough feedback and coaching to actually change the behavior.**

In fact, most difficult behavior is a strength, overused.

- **Directed confidence can become controlling and obtuse.**

- **Reflective and open can become self-focused and conversation monopolizing.**

- **Driven and passionate can become insensitive and abrasive.**

- **Inquisitive and knowledgeable can become disruptive and distracting.**

So, when we work with these (and other) behaviors, we have to understand the very behavior we will be asking someone to change may also be a badge of distinction they wear proudly. Helping people understand the situational requirements and necessity for their strengths is the most compelling job of a coach.

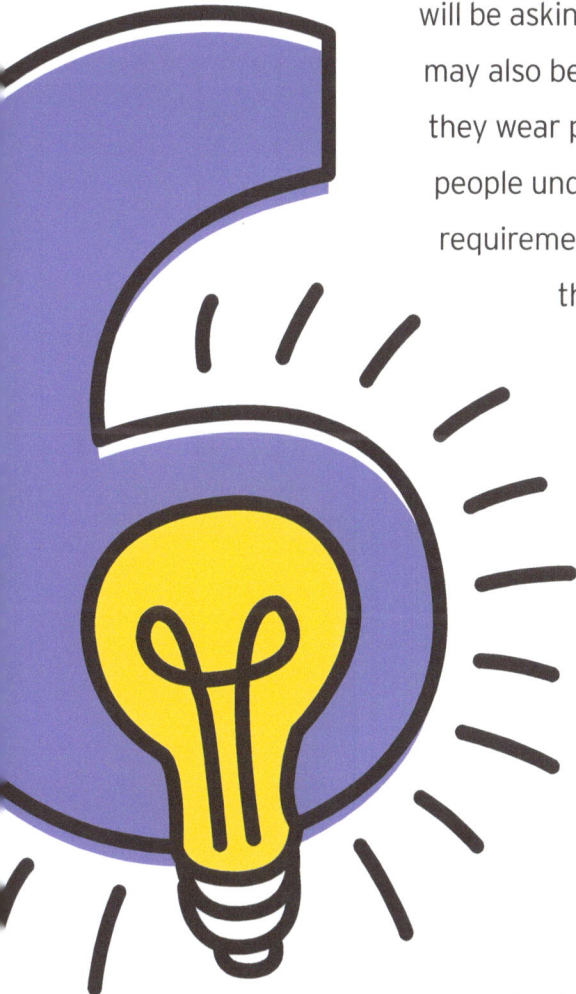

Step 1: Get Clean as a Coach

You have your own assumptions and judgments about the 'difficult' person's behavior. While you may have a lot of evidence to support your judgment, there is no place for your opinion in an effective coaching relationship. You have to 'get clean'; meaning notice and then release your assumptions, so you can really be present for your employee or client. Your opinion isn't relevant. What is relevant is the following:

- **The provable behavior they are or have been demonstrating (use facts here).**

- **The impact of their behavior (again use facts).**

- **The consequence of the behavior not changing.**

- **The client's or employees willingness to make a change in their behavior.**

Your opinion or assumptions play no part here. Therefore, you may have to work hard to remove them from the equation. In fact, the less connected you can become to the actual outcome you have for the coaching, the better. If you have your own agenda for your client, you will end up interfering. Behavior change is an inside journey. As a coach, you can serve up the information, ask powerful questions, and invite your client to make changes. Ultimately, any and all change, is a personal choice.

Use the included reflective questions to work through your own limited or assumptive thinking before you have your first meeting with the employee.

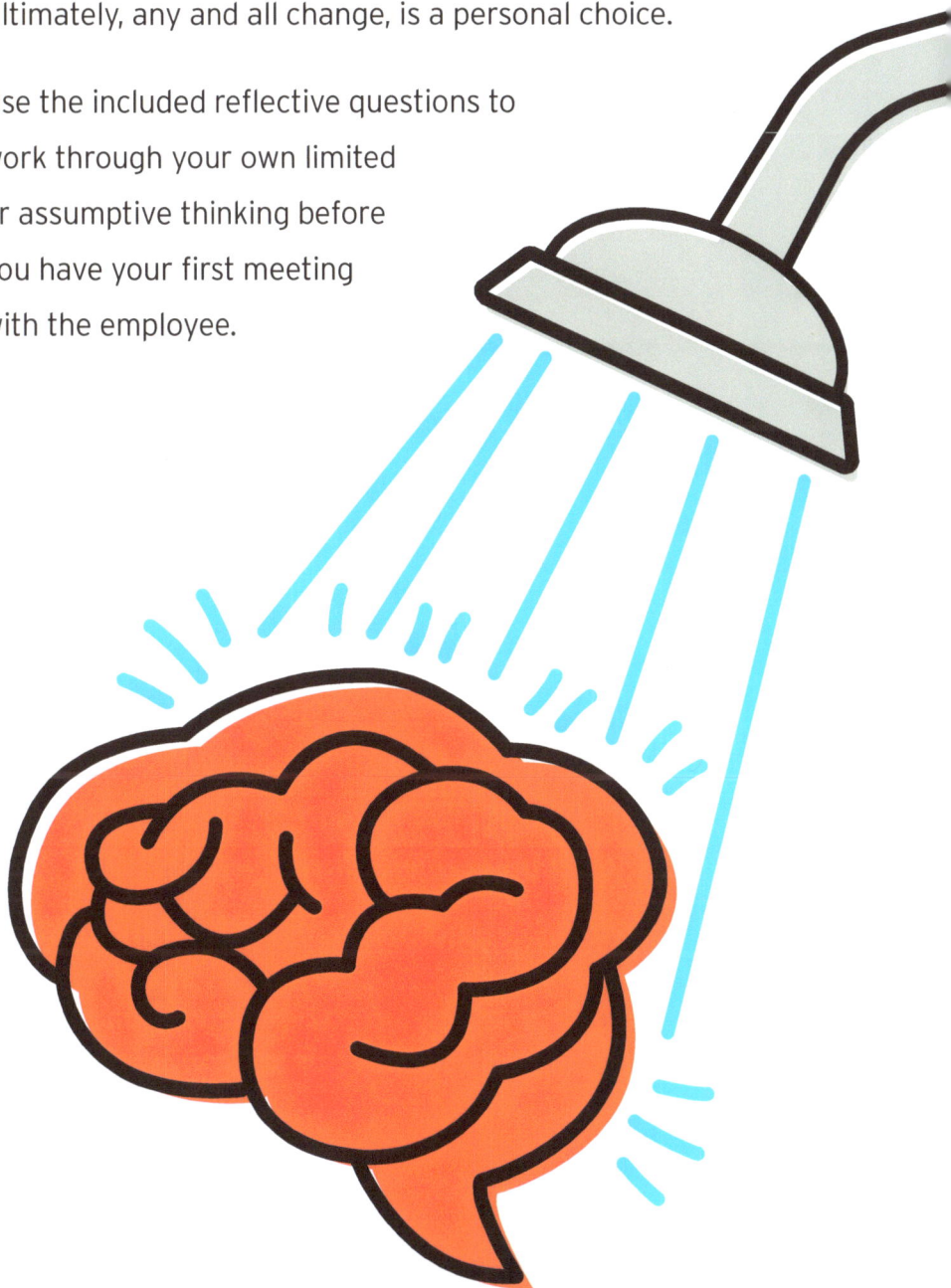

Reflections

- Notice your judgments:

  » *What do you wish this person was or wasn't doing?*

  » *What do you think about this person?*

  » *How do you believe this person is impacting you and your work?*

  » *Are you able to put aside your judgments and listen to this person? Why or why not?*

- Notice your emotional response:

  » *Are you angry?*

  » *Are you frustrated?*

  » *Irritated?*

  » *Disappointed?*

  » *Resentful?*

- Notice your intention:

  » *What do you want to have happen?*

  » *What do you want for this person?*

  » *Who do you want to be in your coaching conversation with this person?*

  » *What is the best outcome for everyone?*

Step 2: Provide Direct, Honest Feedback

As mentioned, when we give feedback we use evidence based in fact. There are no emotions in facts. Facts stand alone. When we remove our thinking about their behavior or their actions, they are simply facts and that is the information we have to share with them. If we get lost in other people's opinions or hearsay, we lose credibility and cannot support our employee in the best way that we could.

For example, if someone on the team is considered to be negative and "toxic", telling them this outright is not effective. That's just someone else's opinion of the individual's behavior. Instead, use specific examples. Such as:

- **In the meeting on Monday, you listed 10 reasons why our new project would fail.**

- **In the conversation we had with Suzy, you told her you didn't think she had what it takes to do the job.**

- **When you walked into the office on Monday, Tuesday, and Friday, you didn't acknowledge anyone and just went straight into your office.**

- **In our meeting on Tuesday, you interrupted John seven times while he was speaking.**

- **When we were meeting with Lucy, you rolled your eyes and sat with your arms crossed.**

In and of themselves, these behaviors stand alone as simply actions someone took. But in summary, they paint a picture. And that's what we want to do for our clients. Paint the picture of their behavior and how it is leading to the opinions of who they are.

Our behavior has impact. It impacts our own brand, the team, performance, and the organization as a whole. As their coach, you must help difficult people understand the impact of their behavior. As mentioned before, it is very unlikely they have noticed how they are impacting others around them. It is a safe guesstimate that nearly 95% of difficult people have no ill-intent. They just don't have any clue about the "wake they leave behind". Introducing themselves to their wake can be an eye opening and sometimes startling experience. Don't expect that they know. Give them as many specifics as you can.

Lastly, we have to help people know the consequence of the behavior not changing. If anything, this is where most managers fail. They may be able to give specific feedback and they may even tell their employees about how their behavior is impacting others. But they fall short in telling them what will happen if the behavior continues, without change.

Changing behavior is hard. We have to give people a clear picture of what lies ahead if they don't do the work to change. A consequence could be anything from negative impact on their personal brand within the organization, reassignment of a project, demotion, termination, or anything in between. If the difficult behavior is serious enough to warrant specific coaching, then there must be skin-in-the-game for the difficult person or you may not actually see the behavior change.

For Step Two, consider the following reflective questions and instructions for giving direct and honest feedback.

- **Evidence based:**

  » *Know your facts.*

  » *Don't make it up or use hearsay.*

  » *Be specific.*

  » *Stay focused on this step before indulging any additional facts or comments.*

- **Connect individual or organizational impact of their behavior:**

  » *Tie observed behavior to impact.*

  » *Be specific.*

  » *Speak as much in fact as you can, keep emotion out of it.*

  » *Explain potential consequences for the individual or organization if the behavior remains the same.*

- **What are the consequences for:**

  » *Relationships.*

  » *Personal Brand.*

  » *Team or individual performance.*

Step 3: Let them be heard

As mentioned, difficult people often don't know they are being difficult. They must have time and a safe place to work through their thinking and to share their perspective. If you want to best help someone through this process, allowing them to be a part of the discussion is essential. The goal here is to bring them with you, but that won't happen if they are confused or cannot see themselves in their own behavior.

When you let someone be heard, you do so by giving them an opportunity to share their own experience, related to the evidence you share with them.

Be prepared for them to be surprised. Be prepared for them to blame other people. Be prepared for them to be defensive and maybe overly pensive.

It's human nature to do whatever we can to get out of discomfort. Many of us attempt to do this by blaming our behavior on other people's behaviors.

It's so much easier to believe other people cause us to do what we do, rather than accepting we ultimately own our own behavior. If you think back to the model in the beginning pages of the guide, we know behavior comes from our feelings. Our feelings come from our thoughts. So how we act is a result of our own thoughts and emotions. Our actions do not just 'happen' because of what other people say or do.

For some people this is a fabulous discovery! It's refreshing to know we really can manage our own emotional health and actions (and results) in the world. For other people this is really bad news. Especially, if they've spent a lifetime blaming other people for how they behave and the results they have. An extreme example is someone who believes they are just 'this' way because of their father, mother, education, town-they-grew-up-in, etc. Actually, you are 'this' way, because you have thoughts that make you feel a certain way. Those feelings drive your actions and those actions lead to your results. Your thoughts. Your results. No one else is in that equation but you.

Keep the following reflections in mind as you are allowing someone to be heard.

Reflections

- Most people don't know their behavior is difficult.

- Your feedback may shock them.

- They may have never heard it before.

- They may have suspected, but no one has ever approached them directly.

- It's common for people to defend their behavior and blame it on other people's actions.

- Expect it.

- Don't get angry or upset.

- Let them express their thoughts. This will be valuable insight for later.

- Do not over-indulge story-telling and lack of ownership.

- The purpose is to listen without judgment and let them be heard.

- You don't have to believe them.

- You don't have to agree with them.

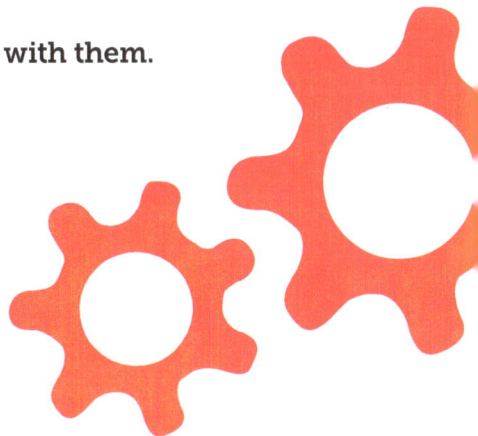

The goal here is to listen with respect and grace. Do not mistake that for believing or buying into their justification. Consider asking your employee/client these questions:

- **Based on the facts I've shared with you, what is your perspective?**

- **What is missing from the information I've shared with you?**

- **Might you see how conclusions have been drawn about you and your behavior, based on the information I've shared with you?**

- **What else do you want me to know about this?**

- **Are you surprised by the feedback?**

- **Why or why not?**

Step 4: Introduce Them to Themselves

All of us are living each moment to moment through a lens that has developed after years and years of experiences. How we each see one another, life, and experiences is uniquely dynamic based on our own life circumstances. When dealing with difficult people, it helps to understand they learned how to interact with other people through their own experiences. And there may have been a time in their lives where the way they react and act were perfectly acceptable and expected.

After we've allowed our clients or employees to be heard, we have to help them meet themselves in a way they may have not done before. Because most difficult people don't know they are difficult, we recommend a process of helping them see how their behavior in the world, has a different impact than they may have considered before. That's why we call it "Introducing Them to Themselves." It's like looking in a prism and seeing another color you hadn't seen before. Even though the color is always there, it just wasn't noticed.

The good news is once we see something we haven't noticed before, we have an opportunity to change how we use our lens and how we see things from now on.

Additionally, most of us believe our behavior is a proper reaction to others' behavior. We focus most of our attention on what someone else did or didn't do, rather than noticing how we may be contributing to the very challenge we are facing.

So when we introduce others to themselves, we want to help them see how their behavior is their own, not because of someone else, AND there are other ways to potentially respond or interact.

- We all have responsibility, for our own behavior, in every relationship and interaction.

- In this step we need to confirm if they are willing to accept this truth; that they have responsibility in every interaction with others.

- What we believe about other people or our circumstances directly impacts our results.

- Ask them:

  » *When you were (insert behavior), how do you think you were feeling? (This may not come to them easily). You may have to help them consider options (happy, sad, worried, or frustrated?)*

- Ask them:

  » *What may have you been thinking about when you did _____?*

  » *What were you making the situation mean?*

- Lead them through the process of discovery.

- Their thoughts and feelings drive their behavior.

Step 5: Invite Them to Notice

Once we notice our thinking ultimately drives our behavior, we can begin to choose how we want to respond, rather than just react. In our work with people who have behaviors that cause challenges on the team, it is imperative they begin to make their own behavior change. It is the only way to make lasting change.

Telling individuals they need to change doesn't work.

Helping them to notice their own behavior and then make a choice about how they want to behave is how we change long-standing habits and patterns.

When we invite our employees or clients to notice their own behavior, we want them to pay attention in a way they haven't before. And, it's essential they do so without judgment or fear.

It's likely there are triggers for them that (up until now) have led them to particular reactions. Whether they are direct, aggressive, dismissive, rude, etc. What we want to do with them in this step is help them start to notice their own behavior **while it's happening**. If they notice themselves as they are demonstrating the challenging behavior, then we can help them understand what they are thinking and feeling that is triggering the behavior.

As they notice they will also be able to pay more attention to what happens around them as a result. Do people retreat or get passive? Do others argue and resist them? Do people roll their eyes or smirk at one another? How is their behavior affecting the team, the meeting, the project, etc.?

- What is the impact of their behavior?

  » *Invite them to see their behavior through the perspective of others.*

- How might they notice this behavior in themselves in the future?

  » *Can they connect to their thinking?*

  » *Can they connect to their feelings?*

  » *Can they notice their own behavior?*

- You cannot change your behavior if you:

  » *Aren't interested or willing to change, AND*

  » *Don't change the way you choose to think about your circumstances and/or other people.*

- You cannot change what you don't see or notice.

  » *Inviting them to notice may take some time.*

  » *It's okay to have them do this work for a while.*

  » *The more powerful the belief, the more commitment is required from the coach and the coachee.*

Step 6: Invite them to Change and Ask for Permission to Practice

Once we help our difficult clients or employees notice their own behavior, then it's time for a change. But, if change happens in a vacuum it may not be seen or experienced (by others) as authentic.

For that reason, we always recommend clients tell others they are working on changing (insert behavior here) and they would like permission from their colleagues to practice the change.

For example, you may be working with a client who talks too much, doesn't listen, and tends to tell everyone what to do. You've followed the previous six steps and the client recognizes how he/she has been acting can be ineffective at best and alienating at its worst. Your client needs to tell his/her teammates that he/she will be working on changing the 'telling' behavior and would like their help as the client moves through the process of change. The client may ask them to remind him/her if he/she starts over-talking or if it appears they aren't listening.

Engaging others in the change process is a powerful way to lower barriers and put people on the same side of the challenge, rather than at odds with one another.

But if your client doesn't ask for permission and just starts to make behavior change, it's very likely others will wonder what the heck is going on and question the authenticity of the change.

This step requires a lot of vulnerability from your client. It isn't easy. But, if your client really wants to make the change, the more people supporting and working with the client, the better!

- They must ask others for permission to make the change.

- Invite them to acknowledge their previous behavior and its impact.

- Apologize if necessary.

- Ask for ongoing feedback and reminders as they work on the change.

- Role play with your employees or clients on how they will have the conversation with their teammates. Don't assume they know how to do this.

- Set up a plan for regular check-ins on progress.

- Celebrate and recognize wins however small or large. Changing behavior is hard work. When our employees and clients do the hard work that is required to make substantive change, we need to make extra efforts to truly recognize their diligence!

Summary

Working with difficult people is one of the most gratifying roles you can play as a coach. Small improvements in behavior, can lead to huge gains within a team or organization. We believe the majority of people who are categorized as difficult do not intend to be. As a result, our hope is you approach their challenging behaviors with an open mind and new tools to glean richer, more powerful results.

But, sometimes the work we do with our clients or our employees doesn't work. They may not be willing to make the changes necessary to improve their relationships and impact on their teammates. If that happens, then there must be a reasonable consequence (as communicated in Step Two). Without the consequence, the behavior will continue AND it may result in others adopting similar challenging or destructive behaviors as well.

To coach the difficult person, follow these six steps:

Step One: Get Clean as a Coach

What you think about comes about. So make sure your judgments are left behind in your work with these clients or employees.

Step Two: Provide Direct, Honest Feedback

Nothing can happen until we tell people the truth.

Step Three: Let Them be Heard

Create room for more than one perspective.

Step Four: Introduce Them to Themselves

We have to see WHO we are in the world if we
are going to change our results and impact.

Step Five: Invite Them to Notice

Once we have tools to pay more attention,
we can start to notice what we haven't seen before.

Step Six: Invite them to Change and Ask for Permission to Practice

Change won't happen miraculously, there must be effort
and focused attention on behavior change to make a
lasting impact.

Helping others change behavior is an investment in time
and in the relationship. The work included in this guide
is intended for those managers and coaches who truly
believe people can change. Trust between you and the
'difficult' person is implied. Take your time with this effort.
Be patient. And above all else, hold the space for them to
believe enough in themselves to make meaningful change.

www.ingramcontent.com/pod-product-compliance
Lightning Source LLC
Chambersburg PA
CBHW041718200326
41520CB00001B/157